CW00520346

FOR THE LOVE OF COOKING
Chef Tao, a Memoir

FOR THE LOVE OF COOKING, Chef Tao, a Memoir © Carmen Bardeguez-Brown
All rights Reserved

ISBN: 9780578281131

I want to thank memoir writer and consultant Charlie Vazquez for his support in helping me structure the process of writing the memoir and Don Linder for his editing and insightful suggestions.

Carmen Bardeguez-Brown

Book design by Marrowstone Design

FOR THE LOVE OF COOKING
Chef Tao, a Memoir

Written by
Carmen Bardeguez-Brown

Recipes by Chef Tao

Pictures and Photographs
by Chef Tao and Carmen Bardeguez-Brown.

For the Love of Cooking is a story of a young Thai who became dangerously enamored with the life of the streets. Radically changed his life path as he chose love over hate, family over turf; and decided to embrace his ancestral Thai culture and became an International Chef, a Thailand Iron Chef competitor, and the successful owner of his restaurant Chef Tao.

His restaurant is between several ancient Buddhist monasteries in the old city of Chiang Mai. Chef Tao's culinary mission is to provide an authentic cultural experience filled with the robust and delectable flavors representing Thailand. His Buddhist beliefs and love for his family influence his cooking approach, *Each dish is prepared as if I'm cooking for my mom and grandmother.*

Chef Tao's memoir is captured in a series of interviews conducted by Carmen Bardeguez-Brown.

Written by Carmen Bardeguez-Brown

Recipes by Chef Tao

Pictures and Photographs by Chef Tao and Carmen Bardeguez-Brown.

We dedicated this book to our families and friends. May this memoir lighten up your hopes and dreams as you seek enlightenment of your Buddha & Christian nature.

CHEF TAO

CARMEN

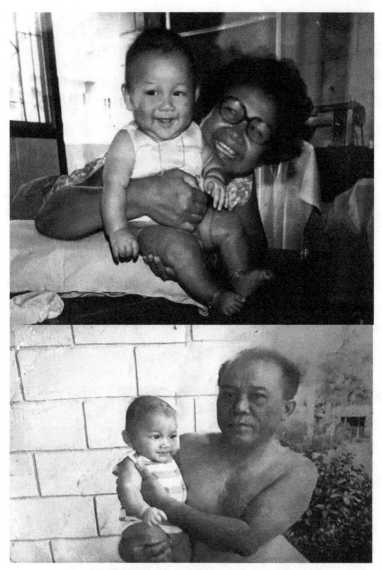

Chef Tao and his grandmother and Grandfather

Chapter 1
Chiangmai
Green Curry-Kaeng Khiao wan

Grandma woke me up very early to help her organize and prepare the ingredients that she would use to cook the daily meals. The green curry was her favorite. I was young and liked to go to clubs at night and enjoy the street life. On some days, Yay wakes me up early to ask for help in the kitchen. She knew I had gone to sleep late, but she did it anyway. I never said no to her. I loved her, and she needed my help, so I always said yes, even if I'd only had just a few hours of sleep.

Grandma used only raw ingredients in her cooking, including making the coconut milk. She used the brown coconut to extract the meat from the hard shell.

Chef Tao's grandma, or Yay, taught him to make the silky white coconut milk used in Thai dishes. Making coconut milk from scratch is a tedious task that he did many times for her. He accompanied her to the market and watched as she selected the fresh produce used for her daily cooking. He carried the bags full of fresh produce to her kitchen. Yay also taught him how to use the mortar and pestle. Chef Tao said that his grandmother had weak wrists and asked him to blend the fresh ingredients the traditional Thai way by using the mortar and pestle; this is a technique that he has fully embraced in his cooking routine. He enjoyed pounding the fresh ingredients with force and rhythm. Who can forget his lively performance as he blended the ingredients in the mortar and pestle during the "Iron Chef" competition season 7, episode 36?

I was young, and at that age, cooking was not my main interest.

The cooking preparation processes that he learned from his grandmother played a pivotal role in his journey to become an International Thai Chef. He was an active and unruly young man barely interested in the strict culture of Thai traditional schools. He ignored his family's pleas, and not even his own mother's professional educational background seemed to curtail his destructive path. What he wanted most during his young life was the adrenaline-induced street fights. His reputation as a fierce opponent propelled him to become a street fighter. He used the skills learned in Muay Thai boxing to control the street turf; he loved the freedom and the power that came with it. He loved the fast-paced and physicality of letting his feelings manifest

Wat Umong

with each punch and win.

But his life was not always like that.

Chef Tao was born in Bangkok. He lived with his mother, father, and sister until he was twelve. He attended The Royal School Panapun Wittayalai, a renowned school in the capital. The family moved to Chiang Mai, and as he said, "that was when everything started." He and his sister experienced the usual newcomer bullying experience at school, which is common when entering a new cultural space. Although they are both Thai, the Thai language of Bangkok is different from the one spoken in Chiang Mai.

Most westerners don't realize that north Thailand, which is composed of the provinces of Chiang Mai, Chiang Rai, and a few others, is quite different from Bangkok, which is in central Thailand. North Thailand was under the Lanna kingdom, which ruled northern Thailand for hundreds of years. The cuisine, language, and many norms and cultural mores are the legacy of the Lanna culture which contributed to his and his sister's adjustment problems.

The ancient city of Chiang Mai has over 700 temples or wats. Some date back to the Lanna kingdom established around the 1200s. Chiangmai became the kingdom's new capital after the king moved it from ChiangRai.

Chef Tao and his sister Toey found themselves in a different cultural environment. Throughout these critical formative years, he was bullied by other kids to the point that his uncle decided to train him in Muay Thai boxing. He wanted Chef Tao to learn to defend himself. The training paid off, but the self-defense training took a different turn as he used his training skills to engage in street fights. Winning street fights became an aphrodisiac that lured him to a life that soon would foreshadow a dangerous dead end.

Wat Chedi Luang

Chef Tao Green Curry

Green Curry Chicken by Chef Tao

- one whole chicken – 1.4 kg. in total weight (ไก่) – I think a free-range chicken gives you the best Thai green curry paste
- 2 cups of water to first boil the chicken
- green curry paste (เครื่องแกงเขียวหวาน) – all of the green
- curry paste below
- 2 – 3 cups of coconut cream (หัวกะทิ)
- 6 – 10 Thai eggplant (มะเขือเปราะ)
- 6 – 10 stems of Thai sweet basil (โหระพา)
- two red spur chilies (พริกชี้ฟ้าแดง)
- 20 kaffir lime leaves (ใบมะกรูด)
- 1/2 teaspoon salt (เกลือ) – or salt to taste when you're
- cooking your curry

For the green curry paste (เครื่องแกงเขียวหวาน)
- 150 grams of Thai green chilies (พริกขี้หนูเขียว)
- one head of garlic (กระเทียม)
- three shallots – small shallots about two tablespoons in total (หอมแดง)
- one thumb-sized chunk of galangal (ข่า)
- five cilantro roots (รากผักชี) coriander
- one kaffir lime – just the peel (ผิวมะกรูด)
- two stalks of lemongrass (ตะไคร้)
- 1 tbsp. white peppercorns
- 1 tsp. coriander seed
- 1 tsp. cumin seed)
- 1 tsp. salt
- 1 tbsp. shrimp paste

Chapter 2
Chiang Mai
Stir-Fried Eel-Pad Phad Pla-Lai Prik Kaeng

Chef Tao at Four Seasons

Chef Tao loved the fried eel that his grandmother cooked.

Like many teenagers, his erratic behavior was as slippery as an eel. He was young and disliked following rules; he was also sad that his father left the family after his parents' divorce. At a young age, he believed that his duty as a young man was to take care of the family. For the first time, Tao experienced the deep suffering of a broken heart. Street fights gave him the space to let out his anguish and confusion. Winning made him feel invincible. Nobody could see his broken heart or feel his pain while he fought in the streets of Chiang Mai.

Signs that are commonly posted around Buddhist temples. This one is at Wat Umong.

Drinking, partying, and going out with girls gave him a sense of power. He experienced emotions too deep for him even to acknowledge them. Like the lotus flower's roots, he was still dwelling in the mud to figure out his life's purpose. Not even the love of his mother and family could soothe his aching heart.

At 17, Chef Tao almost lost his life during one of his regular street fights.

The dagger intended to pierce his heart barely missed him. A fast leg kick movement, or maybe his mother's prayers, diverted the knife that was going straight towards his heart. His right arm was severely wounded, and Chef Tao was saved by a fast reflex, angels, or karma. After that incident, he promised his mother that he would attend a monastery for a month. It was a loving intention that the family hoped would calm his temperament. Maybe it did, or it didn't, but at least those were a few weeks before he was in a safe place.

As a novice monk, he was supposed to follow the monastic regulations, but *"I spent most of the time in the temple playing soccer. I have no idea how the monks put up with me."*

Buddha busts at Wat Umong

Stir fry Eel by Chef Tao

ส่วนผสม
- ปลาหั่นเป็นแว่น ๆ 1 ก.ก.
- กระชาย 2 กำมือ หอม ช่วยดับกลิ่นคาว ได้เป็นอย่างดี
- กระเทียม 6 กลีบ
- พริกสด 6-10 เม็ด
- พริกแกงเผ็ด 2 ช้อนโต๊ะ
- น้ำตาล 1 ช้อน
- น้ำปลา
- ซอสปรุงรส
- ใบมะกรูด 6-10 ใบ
- หอมใหญ่ 1 หัวซอย
- ใบกระเพรา 1 กำมือ

วิธีทำ
ตำพริกแกงก่อนเลย
- ตำกระชาย กระเทียม พริก ให้พอหยาบ ไม่ต้องละเอียด จากนั้น ตำพริก แกงเผ็ดเข้าด้วยกัน พักไว้
- น้ำมันใส่กระทะ ตั้งไฟกลาง ๆ เอา พริกแกงลงผัด จนหอม 3.น้ำเนื้อปลามาผัด ช่วงนี้เติมน้ำด้วย เพราะเนื้อปลากว่าจะสุก จะนาน หน่อย
- ใส่ใบมะกรูด
- พอปลาสุก เติมเครื่องปรุงลงไป แล้วสุดท้ายใส่หอมหัวใหญ่ซอย และ ตามด้วยใบกระเพรา เป็นอันเสร็จพิธี ง่าย แต่อร่อย มาก ๆ

Stir fry Eel by Chef Tao

Ingredients
- Eel cut 1 kg
- Lady finger 200 gram
- Garlic 6 pcs
- Chili 6-10 pcs
- Red curry past 2 Tbs
- Sugar 1 Tbs
- Fish sauce to taste
- Seasoning sauce to taste
- kaffir lime leave 6-10 leaves
- Onion 1 pcs
- Holy basil 1 hand

Procedure
- Pound curry
- Pound lady finger, garlic, chili and leave on the side
- Put oil into wok and put curry past inside
- Put eel in until well-cooked
- Put kaffir lime leave
- Once the fish is cook through, put seasoning into wok with
- onion
- At the last minute add the holy basil

Loy Krathong celebration, Chiangmai

Chapter 3
Papaya salad Som Tam

Papaya salad is so yummy.

I always tasted the love of my mother and grandmother through the food that they cooked for me. That is something that I learned from both, and to this day, every time that I cook, I want my customers to feel the same way. I want them to feel love through the food that I cook. That is my special ingredient, love.

I want my customers to enjoy the love that I put into every one of the dishes that I prepare.

Yay would make a big plate of Papaya Salad for the entire family and always take extra time to prepare one separate dish for Chef Tao. He didn't like food that was too spicy, and she wanted to ensure that he could enjoy the salad the way he liked it. He loved the extra attention that she gave him. *Grandma made me feel special. Her warm embrace and the love that I felt from her made me happy. She just loved me.* Chef Tao's relationship with his grandma directly influenced the love and passion he later developed for cooking.

I have always been a quiet person.

Chef Tao says that he likes to keep his feelings and emotions to himself. Yay knew him well and always showered him with hugs and defended him when his mother lost her temper due to his street behavior antics. Maybe, Yay's constant requests for his help in the kitchen help her keep an eye on him. Perhaps it was her way of showing him the love and attention that he secretly craved and, at the same time, exposed him to the passion for cooking that he developed later in life.

A teacher once told Chef Tao's mother that he had two opposite characters—a good one and a naughty one. Chef Tao said that he had to learn to balance both traits throughout his life. *"I know that if I didn't remember to be disciplined. I would get into trouble."* Chef Tao developed a liking and ability to be successful in martial arts. He became a national Tae Kwon Do champion at the age of 17. Right after the championship, Chef Tao opened a Tae Kwon Do school. He was making a lot of money, but the success contributed to the fast erosion of anything related to his academic education.

His mother was concerned and asked him to complete his high school education. He agreed. She was also considering other options to support her son's overall development. His prowess and physicality helped him conquer his temperament, but it would be the love of his mother and grandmother that led him towards his life's passion. His willingness to embrace purposeful discipline in sports and his love and respect for his family helped him redefine how to deal with pain and embrace life's challenges to achieve goals. Like the intense and powerful yet sweet taste of the papaya salad, Chef Tao was quietly learning the skills that, at the appropriate time, would coalesce and guide him toward his life purpose.

Chef Tao's culinary presentation in Beijing

Papaya Salad
Som Tam salad by Chef Tao

นั้นคือส้มตำไทย

•เครื่องปรุง
มะละกอดิบหั่นฝอย 2 ถ้วยตวง แครอทหั่นฝอย 1/2 ถ้วยตวง ถั่วฝักยาว 1/2 ถ้วยตวง (หั่นความยาวประมาณ 1') น้ำปลา 2 ช้อนโต๊ะ
น้ำตาลปี๊บ 1 1/2 ช้อนโต๊ะน้ำมะนาว 3 ช้อนโต๊ะ มะเขือเทศ 1/2 ถ้วยตวง (หั่นครึ่ง)
กุ้งแห้ง 1/3 ถ้วยตวง
ถั่วลิสง 1/4 ถ้วยตวง
พริกขี้หนู 10 เม็ด (ปรับเพิ่ม/ลด ตามความต้องการ) กระเทียมสด 5 กลีบ

•วิธีทำ
- ใส่กระเทียมและพริกลงในครก ใช้สากตำพอแหลก จึงใส่
- กุ้งแห้งและตำต่อไปอีกสักพัก
- ใส่น้ำตาลปี๊บ ตำต่อจนน้ำตาลละลาย จึงใส่มะละกอฝอย,
- แครอทฝอย, ถั่วฝักยาว, มะเขือเทศ, ถั่วลิสง ปรุงรสด้วย น้ำปลาและน้ำมะนาว จากนั้นจึงตำต่อจนส่วนผสมทั้งหมด เคล้ากันทั่ว
- ปรุงรสให้ถูกปากด้วย น้ำตาล, น้ำปลา หรือน้ำมะนาวเพิ่ม รสดั้งเดิมจะมีรสหวาน, เผ็ด และเปรี้ยวพอๆกัน
- ตักใส่จานและโรยหน้าด้วยถั่วลิสง เสิร์ฟพร้อมผักสด (กะหล่ำปลี, ถั่วฝักยาว, ผักบุ้งไทย, อื่นๆ) และข้าวเหนียว ร้อนๆ

Papaya Salad
Som Tam salad by Chef Tao

Ingredients
2 cups shredded green papaya 1/2 cup shredded carrot
1/2 cup sting bean (cut into 1' long pieces)
2 tablespoons fish sauce
1 1/2 tablespoons palm sugar
3 tablespoons lime juice
1/2 cup tomato (wedged)
1/3 cup dried shrimps
1/4 cup peanuts
10 green chilies
5 cloves fresh garlic

Procedure
• Use mortar and pestle to crush the chili and garlic,
• add shrimps, continue crushing.
• Add sugar, continue beating with the pestle, then
• add the papaya, carrot, sting bean, fish sauce, lime juice, tomato, and peanuts. Continue beating until all ingredients mixed well.
• Finally, season with sugar, fish sauce, or lime. The original taste this dish
should be the balance taste between sweet, (pepper) hot, salty, and sour.
• Serve with vegetables (e.g., cabbage, string bean, napa, etc.). Thai people love
to eat Sticky Rice with Papaya Salad. In this case, sticky rice can be served together
with finished Papaya Salad.

Chapter 4
Australia
Pork Basil-Pad Ka-Prao Moo

After high school, Chef Tao applied to attend Chiang Mai University on a sports scholarship. He passed the performance test, but through unclear circumstances, he did not pass the interview.

It was devastating.

His mother decided to send him to Australia. He was only 17, so it was a hard decision. She knew that he needed to learn about the world. He needed to leave Thailand and Chiang Mai to become what he needed to be and accomplish something in this world. She gave him a small amount of money, a few English phrases on a piece of paper, and her love and blessings. His mother wanted him to get the best education possible to live a good life and be responsible. She also wanted him to learn English.

She wanted her son to mature and become the productive man she knew he could be.

Like the bird that forces her young ones from the nest, she needed to let her son fly away towards his destiny. She trusted her motherly love and the guidance of her constant prayers.

Chef Tao arrived in Sydney and took a one-hour local flight to Canberra. It was a trip into the unknown.

I was not afraid to go to a different country, and I respected my mother's decision. In a way, I was ready to embrace the challenges.

Language became one of the first barriers that Chef Tao had to navigate. *I was the only one in the classroom that had to learn basic English. I was the only Thai student at the school as everyone else was a Westerner.* Chef Tao learned to deal with the cultural differences with patience and an attitude of never to take things personally, which he said he learned while training for Muay Thai boxing.

He needed to select an educational major as part of the school's academic requirements, and he chose the culinary track. According to him, it was the one that had the least requirements. One surprise of studying culinary arts was learning how

Chef Tao during his one-month monastic stay

to deal with the mercurial behavior of the Chef's personality and borderline abusive behavior. As he has known throughout his career as a chef, it is something that seems to come with the profession.

Chef Tao needed to support himself, and after a few months, he found a job as a dishwasher in the kitchen of a Thai restaurant near the school. One day, as he washed the dishes, he was impressed by the butcher's focus and agility while cutting the meat. A slight mistake could become an immediate accident. This synchronicity of movement was familiar to Chef Tao. It reminded him of the skills he learned while training for Muay Thai. The butcher's shiny steel gloves enthralled him. At that moment, he discovered an aspect of the kitchen duties that fascinated him.

He asked the owner to let him become a butcher. The owner let him take on the task, but only after he completed his duty of washing the dishes. He enjoyed his new role. Chef Tao cut boxes and boxes of fresh chicken in one day. The extra pay only made the new task even more attractive.

After six months of double duty at the restaurant, the owner noticed and appreciated his patience, discipline, and work ethic, and asked him to become a chef.

One day one of the customers at the restaurant ordered the Pork and Basil dish; on his way out, the client wrote a complimentary note to the Chef. He was elated. Pleasing the palate of a stranger was a new experience. It ignited a passion that had been dormant since his days of helping his grandmother in her kitchen. He worked at that restaurant for one year.

Always searching for a challenge, he decided to explore Japanese cuisine and became a chef at a Japanese restaurant located in Canberra. For two years, Chef Tao received the education that his mother had dreamed for him. He discovered his passion for cooking.

Once Chef Tao returned to Thailand, he decided to do a one-month stay at a wat as a monk. He wanted to reflect on the direction that his life needed to take. Chef Tao had the unique experience of being mentored by the temple's Abbott. He still appreciates it as it is infrequent to be mentored by the head monk.

Pork and Basil by Chef Tao

INGREDIENTS
- 3 tablespoons vegetable oil
- 2 shallots (sliced)
- 7 cloves garlic (smashed)
- 3 Thai bird or holland chilies (de-seeded, if desired, and thinly sliced)
- 1 pound ground pork (450g)
- 1 teaspoon sugar
- 1 tablespoon fish sauce
- 2 teaspoons dark soy sauce
- 2 teaspoons oyster sauce
- 1/3 cup low sodium chicken broth or water
- holy basil leaves (about 1 1/2 cups packed)

Procedure

In a wok over medium high heat, add the oil, shallots and garlic, and fry for 3 minutes. Add the chilies and cook for another minute. Crank up the heat to high, and add the ground pork, breaking it up into small bits and allowing it to crisp up.

Add the sugar, fish sauce, soy sauce, dark soy sauce, and oyster sauce. Stir-fry for another minute and deglaze the pan with the broth or water. Because your pan is over high heat, the liquid should cook off very quickly. Add the basil, and stir-fry until wilted. Serve over rice.

Chapter 5
UK
Thai Chicken Pandan Leaf -Gai Haw Bai Toey

The time at the monastery made him realize that he had found a career that he liked. He decided to apply for a Thai chef job posting at a Thai restaurant in England.

Chef Tao was resolute in making this new opportunity work. He wanted to be the best Chef that he could be, and England became an essential step on his journey of becoming an International Chef. He stayed in England for four years. Two years in London and two years in Bradford.

He made friends with people from India and Pakistan and learned to tolerate the weather and the coldness of the overall English culture. He found it challenging to engage with the English cuisine, which he found bland. *There is a lot of fish and chips. In my opinion, there is not a lot of variety in the English cuisine."*

One dish that stood out during this time was the Thai Chicken Pandan Leaf. Customers were mesmerized by the look and the taste of this "exotic plate." Chef Tao said that people were intrigued by how he used the leaf when making the dish. He had to tell people not to eat the leaf on many occasions. The leaf is used as part of the preparation of the chicken; most people do not eat them. Living and working in England became a significant step of his steadfast resolute toward becoming an International Chef. Patience was finally paying off.

Chicken Pandan Leaf

Chicken Pandan Leaf by Chef Tao

- 500 grams skinless chicken breast fillet, cubed
- 5 coriander roots, cleaned and chopped
- 4 garlic cloves, crushed
- 1 teaspoon white pepper
- 1 tablespoon soy sauce
- 3 tablespoons oyster sauce
- 1/2 tablespoon sesame oil
- Pandanus leaves, cleaned (for wrapping)
- vegetable oil for deep-frying

Ingredients for dipping sauce
- 5 tablespoons sugar
- 2 tablespoons water
- 3 tablespoons soy sauce
- 1 tablespoon black soy sauce
- 1/2 teaspoon salt
- 1 tablespoon roasted sesame seed

Chapter 6
Thailand
Grandmother-Yay

I asked Toey, Chef's Tao sister, about their grandmother and how she saw their relationship.

He was her favorite, Toey told me. Y*ay had five kids, and our mother was the one in the middle and the only girl. He was also the first grandson. Grandma always protected him and pampered him.* I asked Chef Tao about Yay, and he reiterated the same sentiment but in a different, more personal way. *Sometimes mom wanted to hit me because I was misbehaving, and grandma would place herself between us so she couldn't hit me. I loved her so much. She made me feel special. I was the last one to see her alive.*

One day Chef Tao's aunt called him and said that grandma did not wake up. His uncle had called her, but she did not respond to the call. When he arrived at her home, he decided to check on her; he saw her on the floor, looking up at the Buddha statue on the wall. He carried her to the bed and gave her a mangosteen. His mom gave her 2,000 baht to donate to the temple.

The next day she passed away.

Everyone in the family said that she was waiting for me. That grandma wanted to see me before dying.

Toey described their grandma as a big, fat woman with tan skin. She wore her hair short and dressed in the traditional Thai top and Thai skirt. She had an herb and fruit garden in her house near the kitchen to use fresh produce in her cooking.

Toey said that she remembers how grandma would ask her to get the fruit to make the traditional Som-Tam salad for the family. She would cook a big plate for ten family members, but she always had a special dish for Chef Tao. Toey

Yay's kitchen cabinet in Chef Tao's restaurant

said that she would cook three meals every day for the entire family. She is sure that Yay expressed her love through cooking. Chef Tao learned to cook Thai food from Yay, his grandmother.

I learned all of the Thai recipes from my grandmother, not from culinary schools. Many people do not believe me but that is the truth. I learned the Thai cuisine from her and every time that I cook; I do it thinking of her and my mother. I am very careful with the ingredients, and I have a special ingredient which is love.

Maybe all of those years of assisting his grandmother influenced Chef Tao until it all flourished later in his life. Chef Tao keeps a loving reminder of his grandma and her kitchen stories in his restaurant. He inherited her kitchen cabinet, which is on display at his restaurant.

' Chef Pirun ' Thai Chef Instructor

Cooking
School

Four Seasons Resort, Chiang Mai

Chapter 7
Thailand
Thailand Four Seasons Tent de Camp Chiang Rai
Butterfly Pea Flour -Dook-an-Chan bpeeng

I spent four years in England and then returned to Thailand.

I applied for a position as Chef at The Four Seasons in Chiang Rai. This was a great opportunity as I first became sous chef and later Chef of The Four Seasons. I had to supervise and support a staff of over 100 people. It is also the place where I learned to master how to make the Butterfly Pea Flour.

In addition, it's where I started teaching. I used this recipe to teach students because the plant's flower becomes blue at the contact with hot water. You can also change the color to purple by mixing it with lemon.

My students' reactions were always enthusiastic. I used the dark purple flour to make dumplings filled with pork, cilantro, garlic, white pepper and palm sugar. Whenever students ate the dish, I

always got rave reviews because the students were engaged in the cooking process.

In Chiang Rai, I trained over 100 staff members in many hospitality areas like kitchen, gardening, purchasing, and food and beverage preparation. After two years at Chiang Rai, I was offered a contract at the Four Seasons in Chiang Mai.

Butterfly Pea Flour by Chef Tao

Chor Muang (Flower Shaped Dumpling filled with Minced Chicken
ช่อม่วง สูตร
ส่วนผสม

- **Rice plant's flower** ข้าวเจ้า 2 ถ้วยin **Thao Yai Mom Flour 1 cup**
  แป้งท้าวยายม่อม 1 ช้อนโต๊ะ

- **Tapioca Flour**
  แป้งมัน 2 ช้อนโต๊ะ

- **Water 1 cup**
  น้ำเปล่า 1 ถ้วย

- **Butterfly Pea Flour**
  น้ำดอกอัญชัน (หรือสีม่วง 1/2 ช้อนชา)

- 1 ถ้วย **Sweet Radish**
  หัวไชโป้หวานสับละเอียด 1 ถ้วย

- **Garlic chopped**
  กระเทียมสับ 1 ช้อนโต๊ะ

- **Peanut**
  ถั่วลิสงคั่วบดหยาบ ๆ 1 ถ้วย

30

Chapter 8
Thailand
Thailand Four Season - Chiang Mai
Golden Basket-Kra Thong Thong

The General Manager of the Four Seasons asked me to go to Chiang Mai because they needed an Executive Chef to manage and supervise a staff of 500 people in all aspects of hospitality service. I took the position because it helped me grow and help me develop the staff. I had to ensure that the cuisine followed consistent standards. At this location, we served more people and I dealt directly with the directors of Food and Beverage.

This new position also allowed me to travel around the world as Chef De Cuisine. I went to Beijing, South Korea, Bangkok and many other places. I also became a celebrity chef which allowed

me to represent the cuisine of the hotel all over the world.

In Chiang Mai we had the Golden Basket dish which was very popular. It is a recipe that needs a lot of detailed preparation.

Chef Tao's Golden Basket

Golden Basket Krathong by Chef Tao

Krathong Ingredients (Minced Chicken and Sweet Corn in Crispy Golden Cuo)

- Rice Flour
- แป้งข้าวเจ้า 1/2 ถ้วย
- All-purpose flour
- แป้งสาลีเอนกประสงค์ 1/2 ถ้วย
- Egg yolk   ไข่แดง one ฟอง
- Lime water
- น้ำปูนใส one ถ้วย
- Coconut milk
- หัวกะทิ4 ช้อนโต๊ะ
- Salt
- เกลือ 1/2 ช้อนชา
- Coriander root
- White pepper
- Garlic
- Chicken diced into 250-gram pieces
- Pea / carrot / corn
- Sesame oil one teaspoon
- Oyster sauce one tablespoon
- Soy sauce with one tablespoon of sugar

Four Seasons Chiangmai

Four Seasons Chiangmai

Chapter 9
Dubai
Traditional Thai Food
Chicken Kao Soi

People in Dubai love spices; cumin, cinnamon and star anise are commonly used, and I added the use of turmeric powder in the process of cooking the Kao Soi. My kitchen staff was from all different countries in Asia, and the general manager wanted me to organize them. He wanted a chef that could teach the team how to achieve high expectations and understand the accountability of working in a prestigious restaurant with a world-class reputation. I created a system that ensured that all staff members felt comfortable and professional in the working environment. This is very important. The Chef is not only an expert of fine dining but is also a leader that needs to ensure that the staff can work under pressure, fast, and without complaints to satisfy the standards of the establishment.

Chef Tao's Chicken Kao Soi

In Dubai, I had same responsibilities as in the other restaurants including Head Chef, Celebrity Chef, Executive Chef, and teacher. They added a new title called Specialty of Thai Cuisine. I had 40 staff members and reported directly to the General Manager.

Dubai was exciting. We cooked for the Emirates and many International clients. The weather, Oh my God! They have huge sandstorms, and now, I understand why they wear scarfs. I also noticed that their architecture is quite different from Thailand's. In Thailand, the ceilings are like a triangle, while in Dubai, they are more like a square shape to help to diffuse the effects of the sandstorms.

Chicken Kao Soi by Chef Tao

Ingredients

18 oz. fresh Chinese egg noodles*
• 2 1/2 cups of cooking oil
• 8 small chicken drumsticks (about 2.2 lbs total)**
• 2 cups coconut cream
• 2 cups coconut milk
• 1/2 cup water
• 1 tablespoon palm sugar
• 1 tablespoon white sugar
• 2 tablespoons Thai soy sauce
• 2 tablespoons fish sauce

Preparation

1. Blend the paste Ingredients together and set aside.

2. Over medium high heat, put 1/2 cup of coconut cream into a wok and fry for 3-5 minutes, stirring continuously, until the coconut oil begins to separate out. Add the prepared paste and fry for 1-2 minutes, stirring constantly. Add the chicken drumsticks, water, remaining coconut cream and half the coconut milk. Bring to the boil, add palm sugar along the side of the wok until it melts, followed by the white sugar, soy sauce and fish sauce. Simmer over low heat for about 30 minutes or until chicken is tender. While simmering, if it becomes too dry, you may add more coconut milk or water.

3. Meanwhile heat the oil for frying the egg noodles in a wok over medium heat and when it is at almost smoking point, add 1/2 cup of egg noodles and fry until crispy and just lightly brown (30 seconds). Strain (we recommend the Brass Strainer Skimmer) and set aside.

4. For the chili oil, heat the 3/4 cup oil in a small saucepan and when it is hot add

the chili powder. Stir together and immediately remove from the heat. Set aside to cool.

5. When you are ready to eat, lower the remaining fresh egg noodles into boiling water to cover, separating the strands of noodles as you add them. Boil for 2 minutes, then drain and portion into 4 individual serving dishes. Top with the chicken curry and serve garnished with the crispy egg noodles, coriander leaves and spring onions.

6. Serve along with the accompaniments, which are added to taste. Use only 1-2 drops of Sweet Soy Sauce per portion. Serves 4.

Chapter 10
Bangkok Anantara@Riverside &
Elephant King International Polo Tournament

I was offered to work with the same company in Bangkok to help them developed their culinary offerings because they were sponsoring the Elephant Polo Tournament. They called me and I had to learn to prepare a combination of Polynesian and Thai dishes at the request of the management.

The new position allowed me to expand my experience as an administrator in the different areas of hospitality.

Chapter 11   The U.S.
Maryland – Washington, DC - Miami
Pad Thai

Chef Tao Pad Thai

Chef Tao decided to embark on a new venture and took a contract to work in the United States at a Thai restaurant in the DC metro area. He and his wife moved to the States in 2017. He worked as the chef of an upscale Thai restaurant named Thai Land located in the border of Maryland and DC.

The owner wanted me to create an upscale menu around the concept of local Thai food such as Pad Thai and Tom Yung. Living in Maryland was an interesting experienced and for the first time in my life I had to learn to drive in the snow. Oh my God, it was colder than London, really cold weather and lots of snow. Digging snow to be able to drive to work was not a fun experience.

Snow cleaning…is not fun at all. So, I decided to go to Miami.

Chef Tao with his mother in Florida

In Miami, I was exposed to the Latino culture and food. I love the Ceviche from Peru and Mexican food. I also like the music and the different dances. I decided to venture on my own and opened my own small Thai place. It became popular and soon Discovery in Spanish came to film and do a segment on my place. I was very proud of that achievement. The most popular dish that I sold there was Pad Thai.

Pad Thai by Chef Tao

Ingredients

- **Noodle** ก๋วยเตี๋ยวเส้นจันท์แช่น้ำพอนุ่ม 250 กรัม
- **Shrimp**ı กุ้งสดปอกเปลือก100 กรัม
- **Dried Shrimp** กุ้งแห้งแช่น้ำ2 ช้อนโต๊ะ
- **Tofu** เต้าหู้แข็งหั่นแท่งเล็ก4 ช้อนโต๊ะ
- **Sweet radish** ıหัวผักกาดเค็มหวานสับหยาบ2 ช้อนโต๊ะ
- **Egg**ı ไข่ไก่3 ฟอง
- **Red Onion**ıหัวหอมแดงสับ และกระเทียมสับ2 ช้อนโต๊ะ
- **Vegetable oil** ıน้ำมันพืช✓ freezing   Water   น้ำเปล่า150 มิลลิลิตร
- **Peanut** ıถั่วลิสงคั่วโขลกพอแหลก ถั่วงอกเด็ดหาง และใบกุยช่ายตามชอบ •
- **Sauce Pad Thai** ส่วนผสมซอสผัดไทย
- **Fish sauce**ıน้ำปลา1 ช้อนโต๊ะ
- **Tamarind**ıน้ำมะขามเปียก✓4 ถ้วยตวง
- **Palm sugar** ıน้ำตาลปีบ✓4 ถ้วยตวง
- **Side dish: banana blossom, bean sprout, lime, chili powder**   เครื่องıหัวปลี, ถั่วงอก, มะนาว, พริกป่

Chapter 12
Thailand
New Beginnings-Mai gaan-reem

I only had my chef shirt and two pieces of luggage. My wife was in Miami and called me to tell me that she was not going to join me in Thailand and that she wanted a divorce.

Chef Tao had been invited to participate in a series of cooking TV shows in Thailand and was planning to return to Miami, but life forced him to take a personal detour. He decided to stay in Bangkok and avoid social interactions with everyone including his family. For the second time in his life his heart had been broken by someone he loved.

After a few months, his mother called him and asked him to come to Chiang Mai because she thought it was time for him to move on. Reluctantly, he decided to go, not knowing that a new pathway was luring him back to the ancient city. Like the lotus flower opening, a new spiritual journey was about to transform his life.

Chapter 13
Chiang Mai
Chef Tao Restaurant

Chef Tao went to Chiang Mai to check out the restaurant location that his mother had identified in the Old City. The restaurant owner wanted to sell the place and retire, and Chef Tao's mother thought that her son might be interested in the opportunity. He fell in love the moment he saw the site. Was it the beautiful Bodhi tree that captured his attention? Or the open space that welcomed the customers after walking through the ancient city and visiting the surrounding temples?

He immediately identified the space that would become the herb garden. The restaurant is close to his former school - the same school that he attended when he was young, where he experienced bullying, where he experienced all those tumultuous years of trying to figure out who he was and who he would be in life. It seemed that life was coming full circle.

A new dream was born, and he took the challenge of designing and creating every detail for a place that would represent his whole experience as an International Thai Chef. His strong Buddhist spiritual beliefs and love for his family were the foundation of this new enterprise. This was the opportunity of a lifetime, and he would embrace it with all his heart and soul. The new restaurant needed a name. His family engaged in the process of finding a name that could showcase his experience and make it his own. After a series of deliberations with his sister and cousins, everyone agreed that the restaurant should have Tao's nickname. And so was born Chef Tao Restaurant. The restaurant would have a chef's garden, a section for teaching classes, and a chef's table. It seems that dreams do come true if you work towards achieving them.

Chef Tao and his mother in Washington D.C

Chef Tao at his restaurant

Epilogue
Cooking Lessons for Life
Chai-nai-gaan-tam-aa-haan chii-wit

I want to share my life journey so that young Thai men can see me as someone that achieved success through discipline and the support of my family. My family gave me unconditional love, Muay Thai Boxing gave me patience and discipline, and the Buddhist practice connected me with my Buddha nature.

My goal in life is to always be strong and serve with love and dedication. Everything in life is possible if you work hard and discipline yourself. I want my daughter to be proud of me and my family to be happy.

I tattooed my mother's name and my family name on both of my arms. I also always carry a chain with Buddha and my grandmother's picture. You always need to love and support your family. Then, you will always be the best that you can be.

Thai Cuisine and Traditional Medicinal purposes

I noticed that in the United States, most chefs use salt and pepper for seasoning. They don't use spices. It doesn't seem to be a common practice. For example, this cabbage dish that I prepare for you is very simple to make. You add a few pieces of pork and soy sauce and let it simmer for a while, and the natural sweetness of the soy and a few pieces of pork complement each other and add flavor.

In Thailand, we try to use only ingredients that are good for you, and I learned from Yay to always use fresh ingredients from the garden. A very popular dish is shrimp sauté with onions and red Chili - nothing else. I'm not a doctor, but many of the ingredients that I regularly use in my cooking are traditional Thai foods that people promote overall health.

Chef Tao's Favorite Thai Cooking Ingredients

Green Thai eggplant
Green and red Chili
Garlic
Galangal
Ginger
Cilantro
Thai Basil
Coconut
Lime

Supporting the Community During Covid -19 Pandemic

The End
Gaan-sin-sut

Or just the beginning of a new journey…

**If you visit Chiang Mai, don't forget to stop by Chef Tao's restaurant.
It is a must!**

**169 Soi Ratchapakinai
Mueang Chiang Mai
Thailand**

A New Beginning …

Artistic Bio

Carmen Bardeguez-Brown is a Puerto Rican-Nuyorican poet. Her work is showcased in the documentary: Latino Poets in the United States by Ray Santiesteban. She has read at The Nuyorican Poets Café, The Fez, Mad Alex Foundation, Smoke, The Soho Arts Festival, Long wood Gallery, The Kitchen, The Bowery Poetry Club, The Boricua College Poetry Series, Governor Island Poetry Festival, Harvard University, Bronx Music Heritage Center, Greenlight Bookstore, Se Buscan Poetas Poetry Reading Series and many other venues. Some of her work has been performed by Felipe Luciano's Poets' Choir, Butch Morris Conduction series, Cantieri del Contemporaneo Poetry like Bread International Video collaboration, and many more.

Her work has been published by magazines such as *Gathering of The Tribes, Long Shot, 2 Horatio, Literary Anthology #1-3, School Voices, Long Shot, Fuse, Rutgers Gallery at New Brunswick, Phatitude Cultural Magazine, Woman Writers in Bloom online magazine, La Pluma y La Tinta Nuyorican Poets Writers* Vol.1 edited by Dr. Nancy Mercado, Xanath Caraza *Poetry Blog and On the Seawall online Poetry Magazine.* Her poems are in various anthologies such as *Aloud Voices* from the Nuyorican, Manteca an Afro-Latino Poets in the United States; I Can't Breathe, Musings in the time of the Pandemic. Ms. Bardeguez-Brown has five poetry books: *Straight from the Drums, Dreaming Rhythms: Despertando el Silencio, Al Otro Lado del Mundo* collaboration with Julio Cesar Paz, *Meditation on Love, Dancing, Loss and Forgiveness, Three Poets* a collaboration with Marlena Maduro Baraf and Julio Cesar Paz.

Ms. Bardeguez- Brown received the 2020 Latina 50 Plus Lifetime Achievement Award for her contributions to Latino Literature in New York.

Twitter https://twitter.com/BardeguezBrown
https://cbbpoetry.wordpress.com/